WILD STARBURSTS
COLORING BOOK
for everyone
Volume 1

L. Saint-Saenz

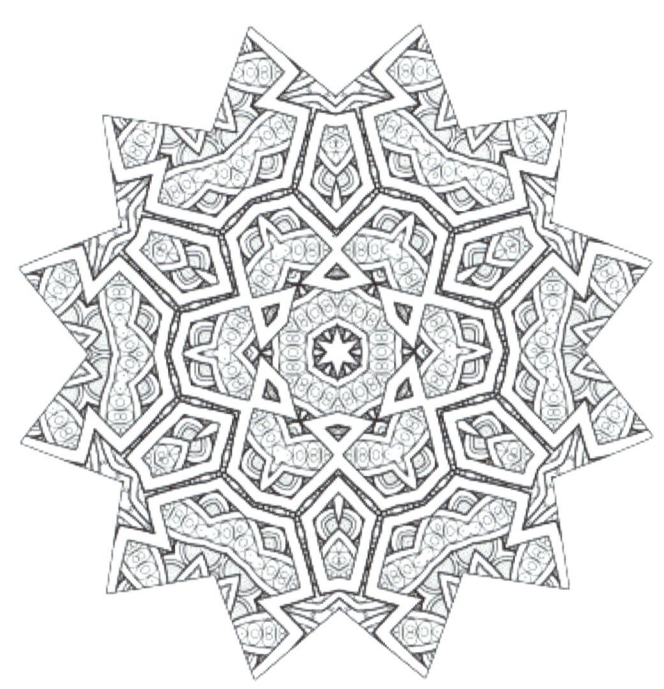

25 Wild Starbursts Designs to Color

Featuring 25 geometric intricate line drawings of diverse patterns, this collection is for everyone who loves to color. These designs provide endless opportunity for experimentation with color and technique.

The imaginative patterns and borders give each design a polished appearance.
Specially designed for experienced colorists, coloring books offer an escape to a world of inspiration and artistic fulfillment.

You will get hours of enjoyment and stress relief as you enhance the designs with colored pencils, markers, and other art media. Considered beneficial to all ages, coloring has been proven to generate wellness and quietness, as well as to stimulate the brain areas related to the senses and creativity. We present this book as one of several coloring books. These artistic drawings offer complexity to engage the brain, but also simplicity, in that there are no rules or even guidelines.

Copyright © 2017
by L. Saint-Saenz

ISBN-13: 978-1975950101
ISBN-10: 1975950100

All rights reserved. No part of this publication may be copied, reproduced in any format, by any means, including scanning, photocopy, electronic or otherwise, without prior consent from the copyright holder of this book.

UNDERSTANDING COLORS

COLOR WHEEL

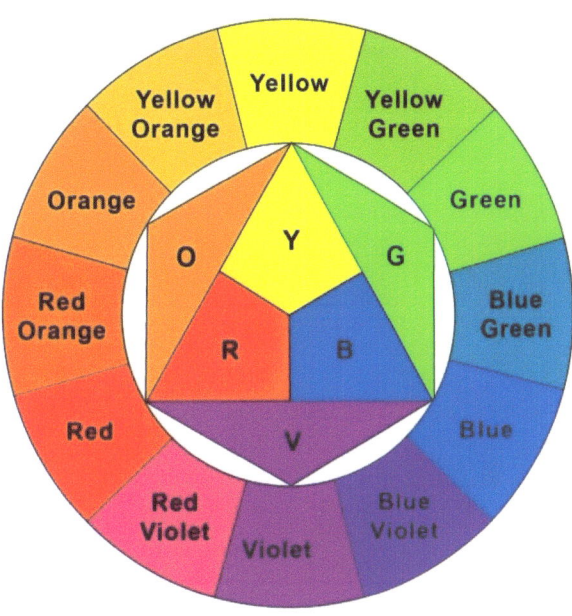

Most Common Color Schemes

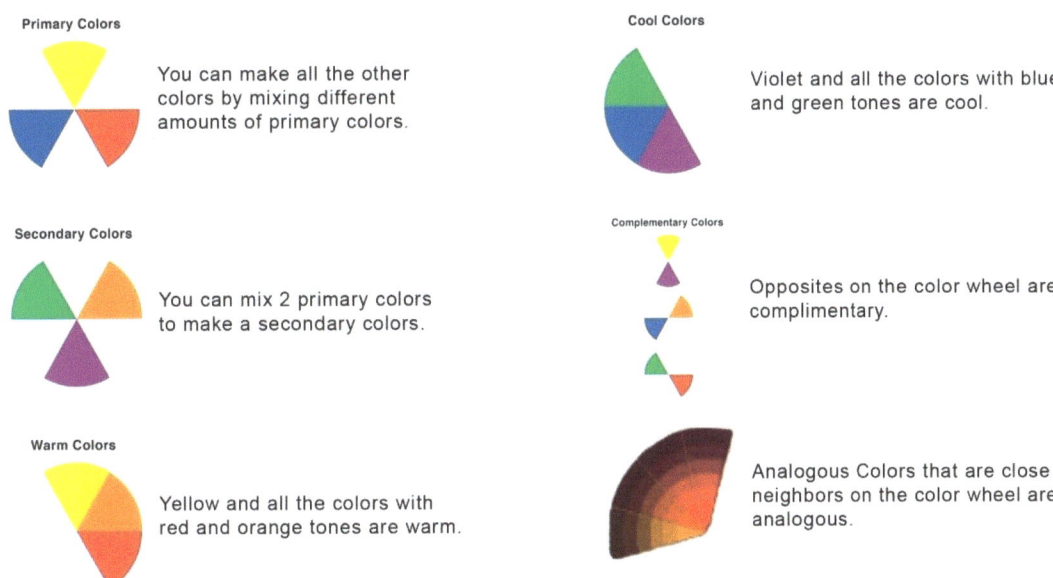

Primary Colors
You can make all the other colors by mixing different amounts of primary colors.

Secondary Colors
You can mix 2 primary colors to make a secondary colors.

Warm Colors
Yellow and all the colors with red and orange tones are warm.

Cool Colors
Violet and all the colors with blue and green tones are cool.

Complementary Colors
Opposites on the color wheel are complimentary.

Analogous Colors that are close neighbors on the color wheel are analogous.

Rainbow-Using primary and secondary colors placed in order from the color wheel, you can make a rainbow.

Intermediate-Is a color term you need to know. It is the color in between the primary and secondary colors on the color wheel.

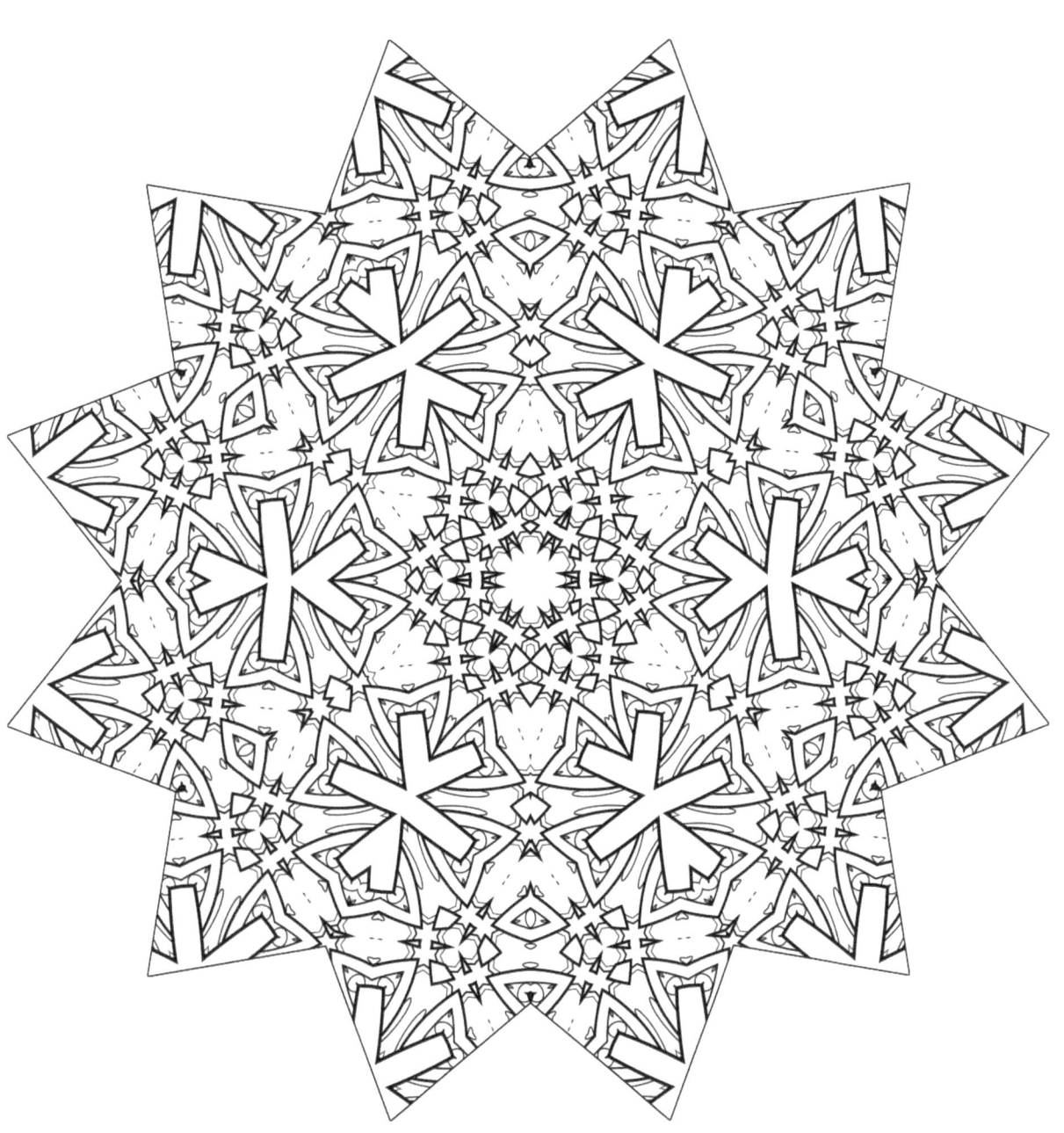

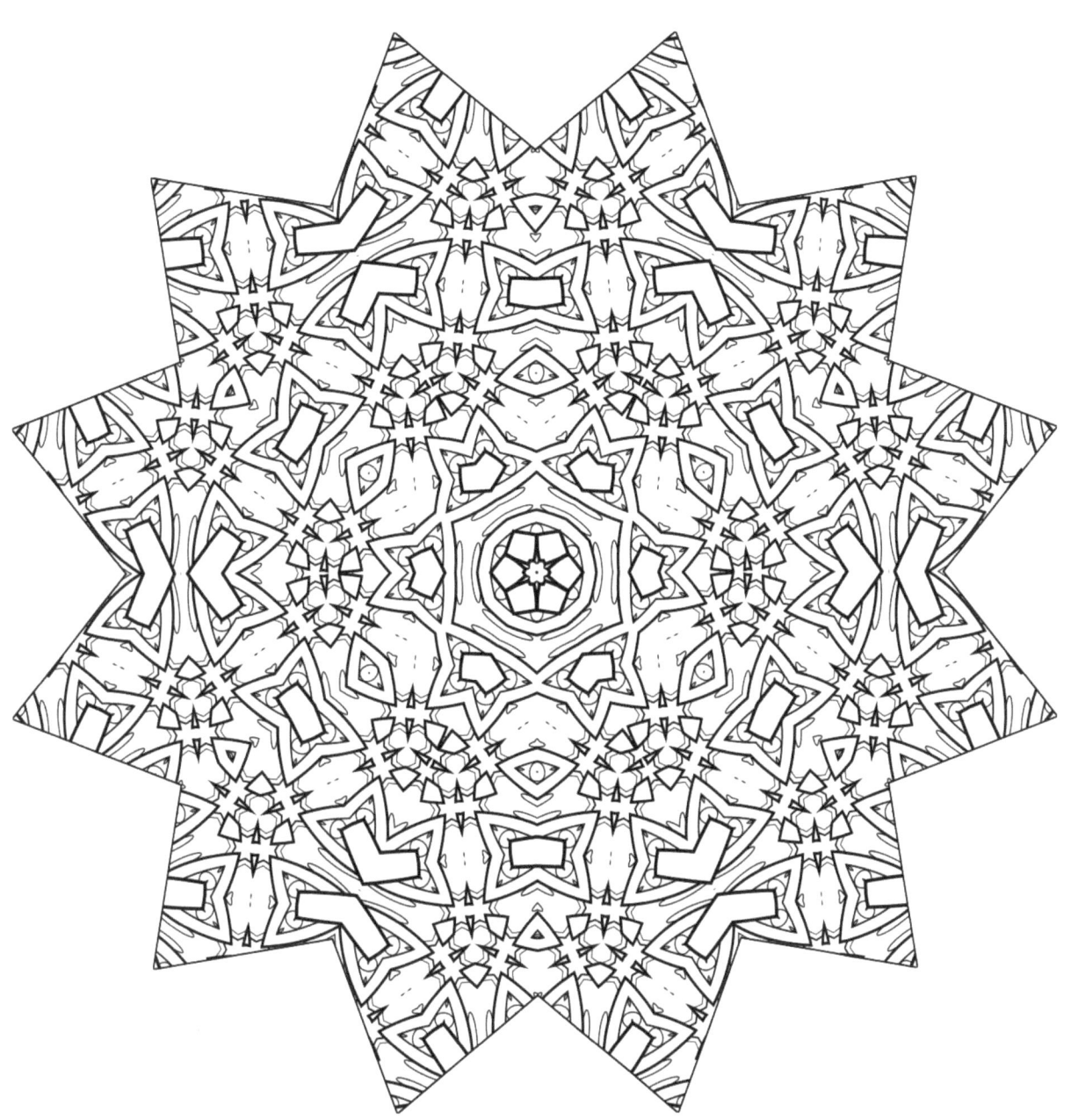

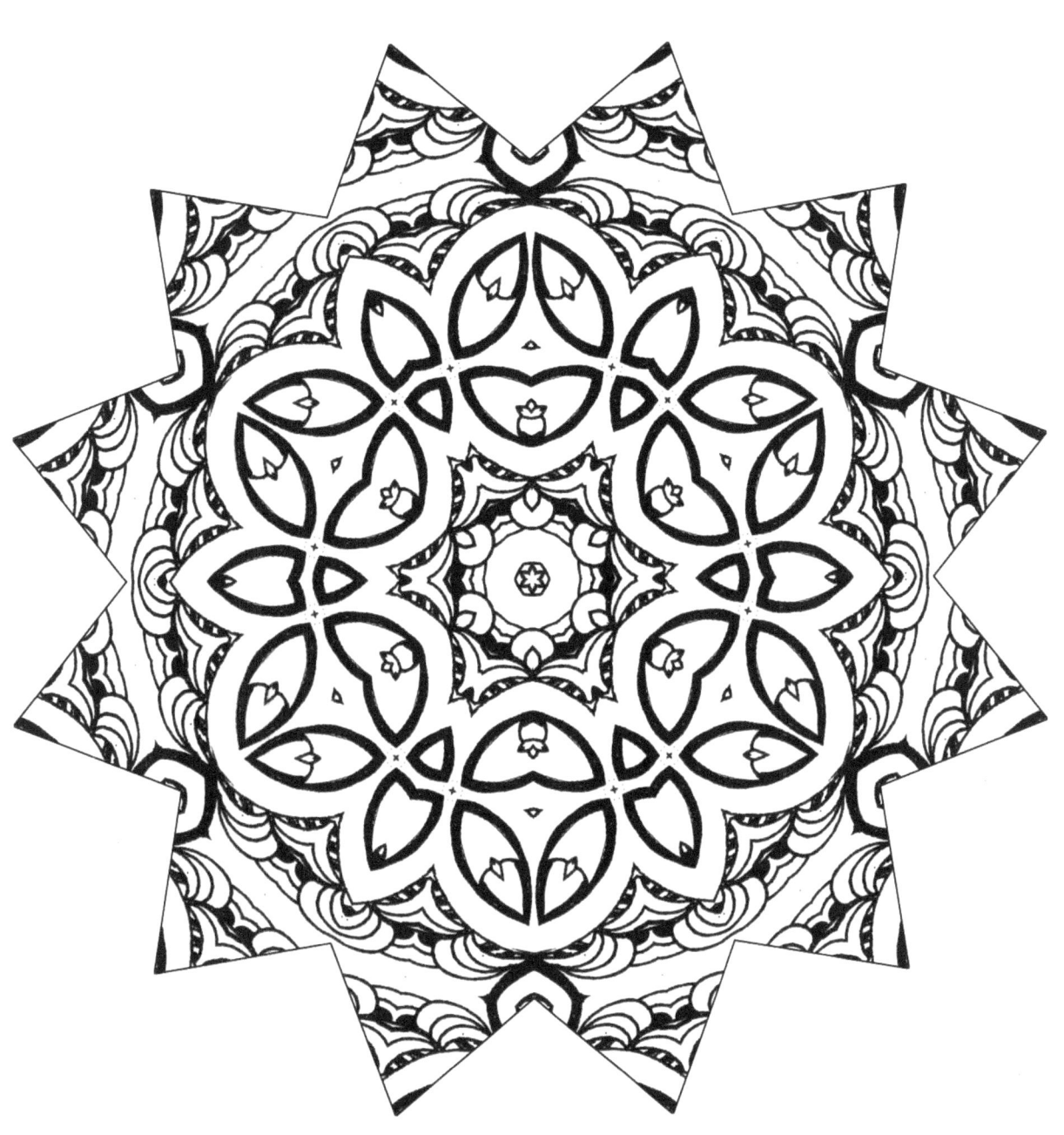

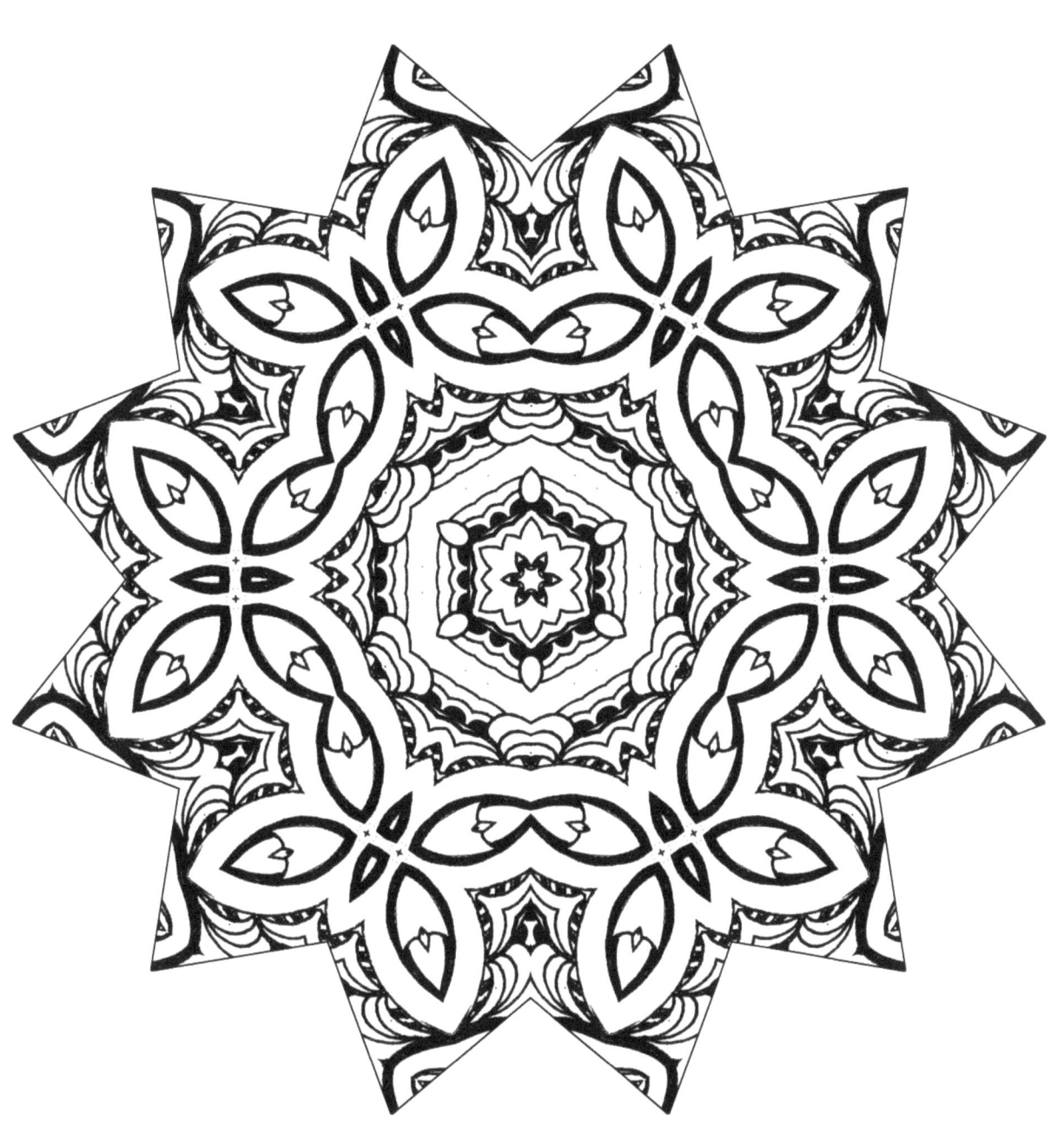

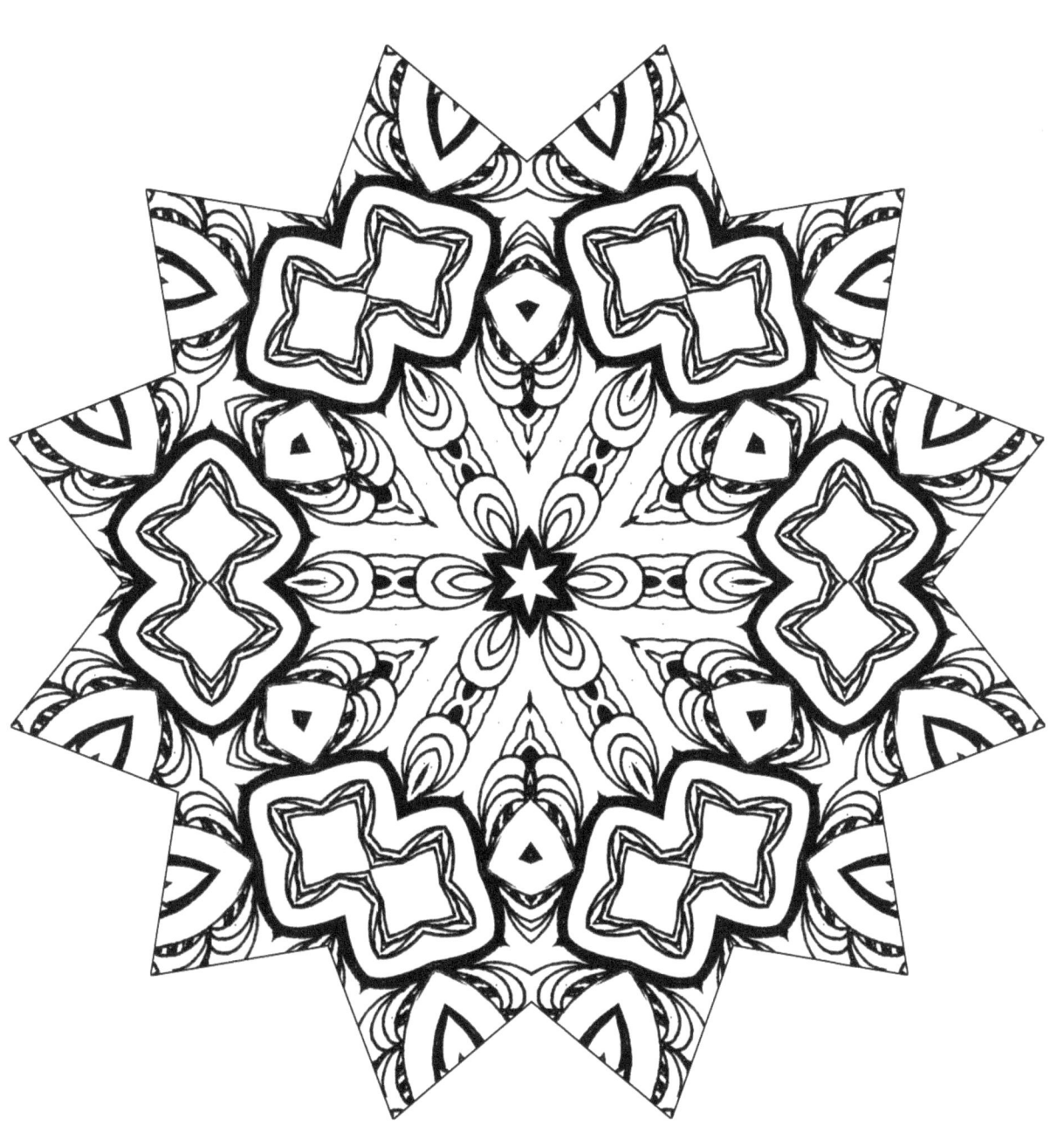

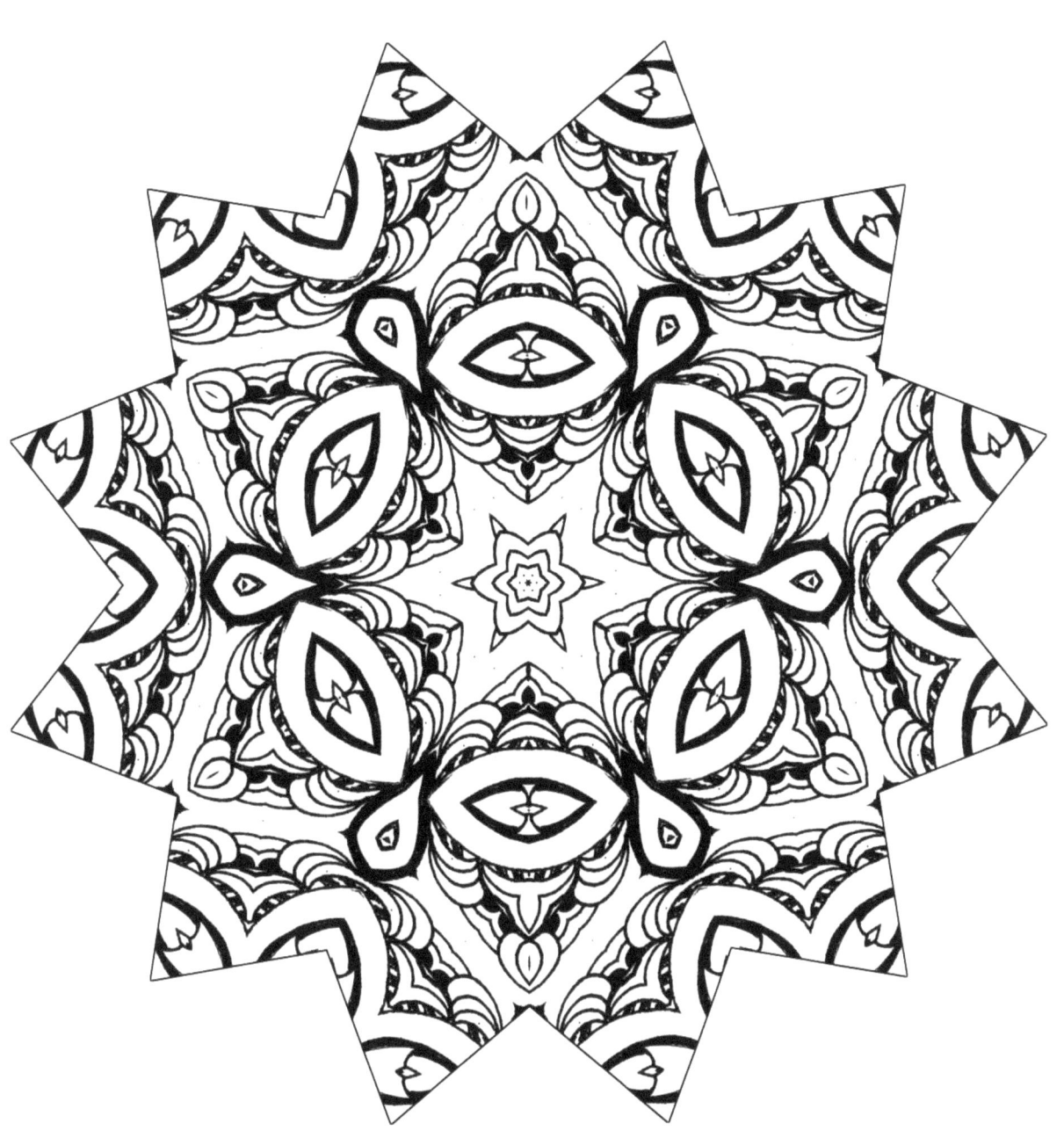

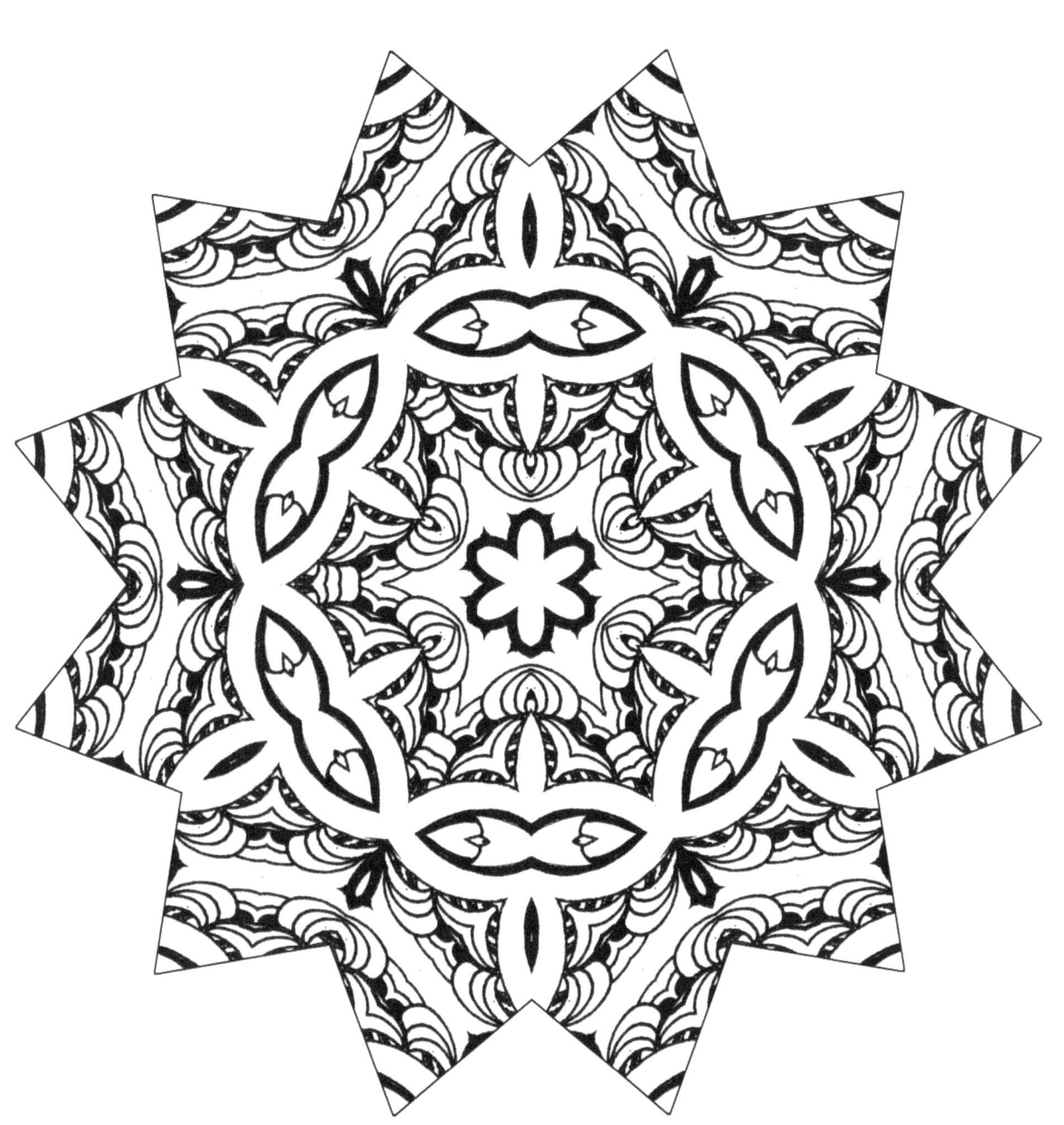

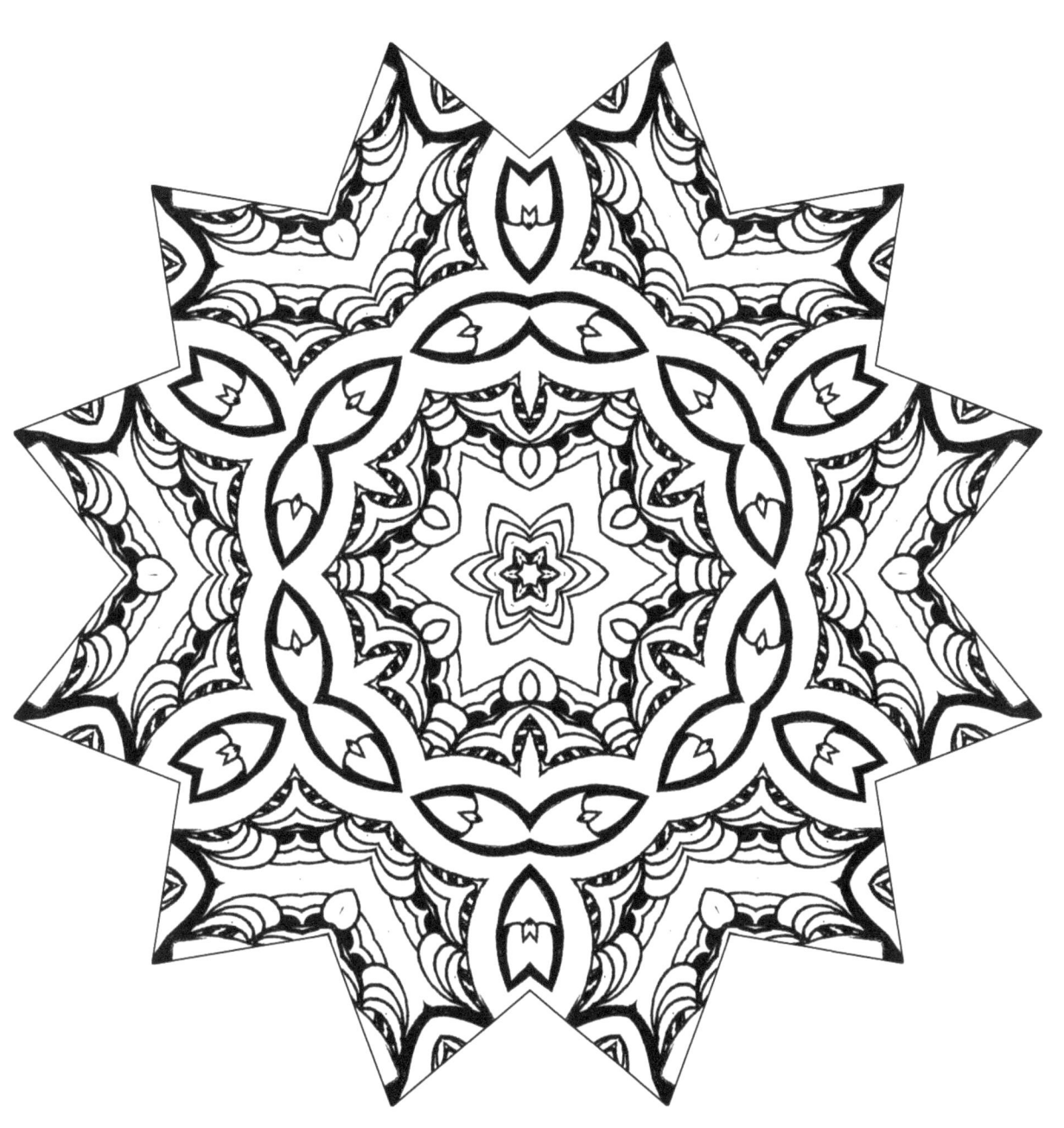

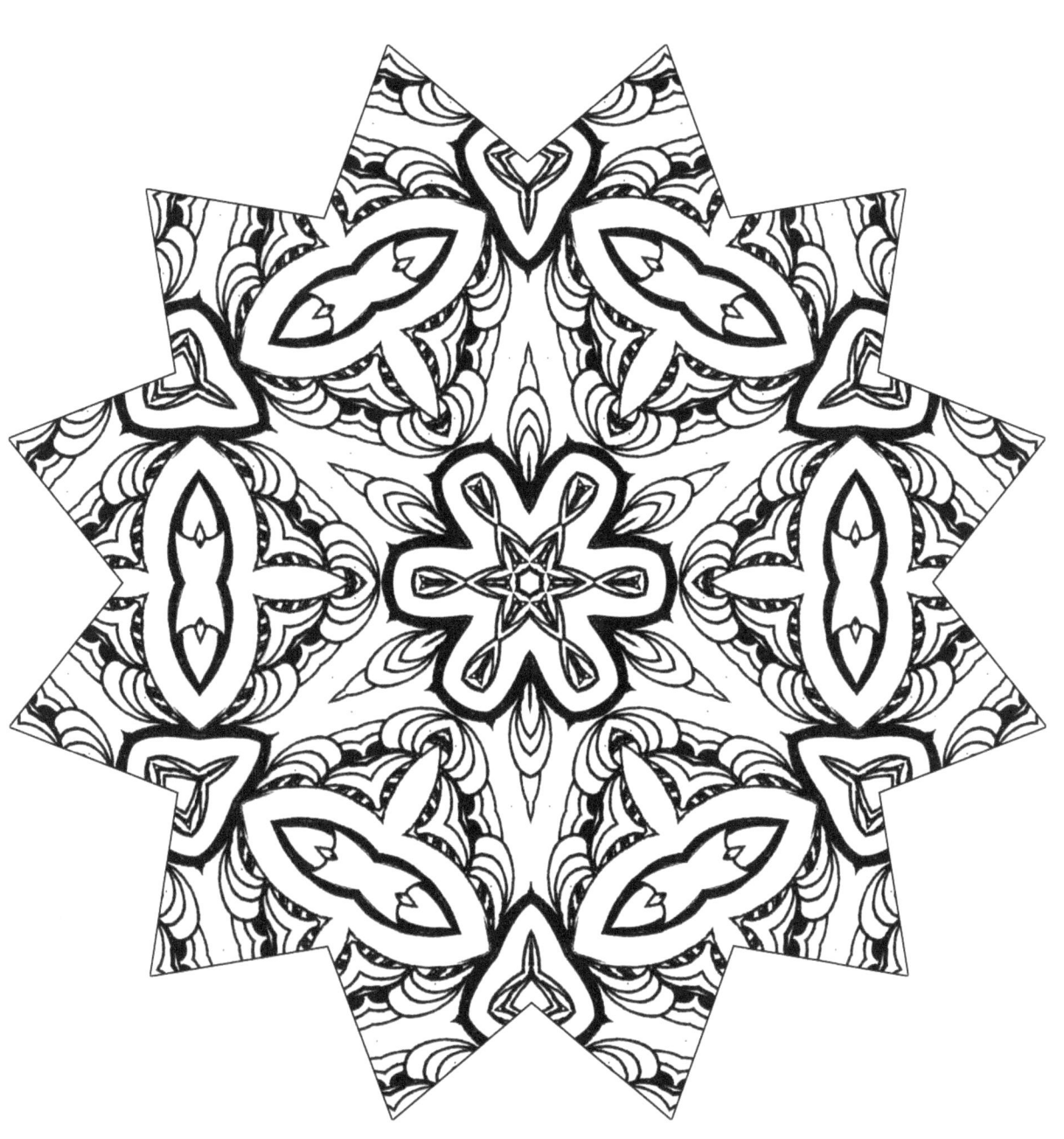

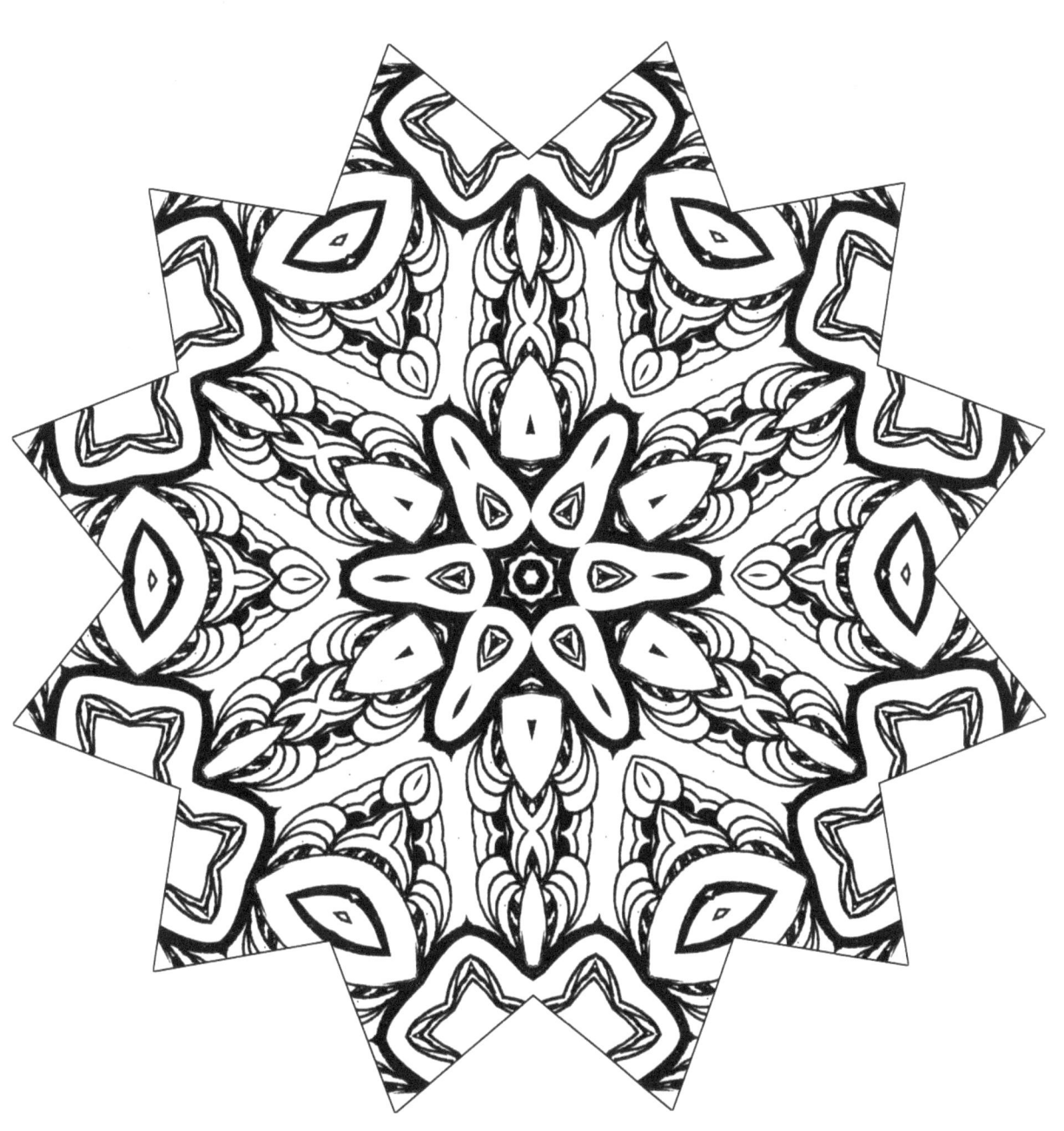

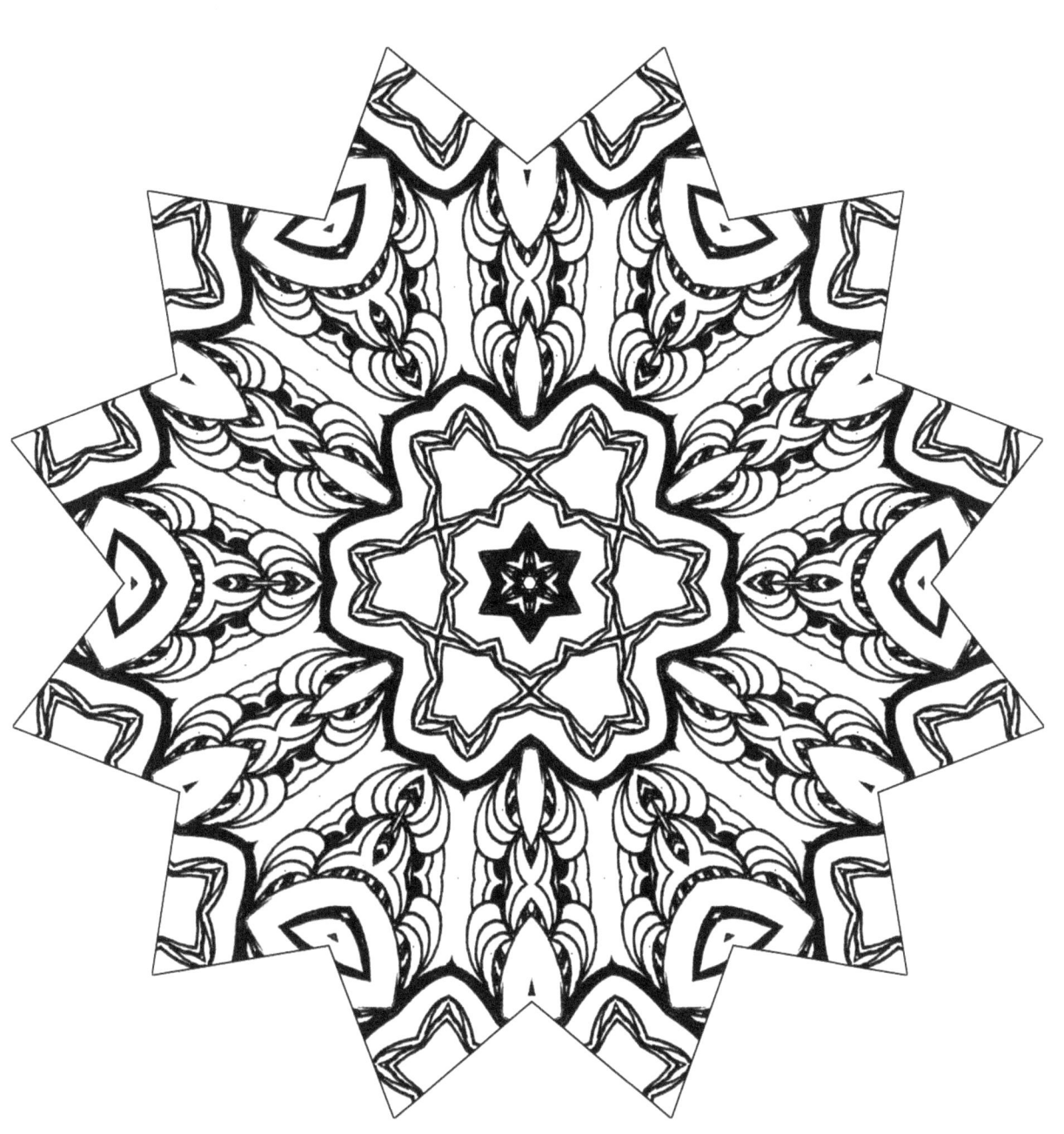

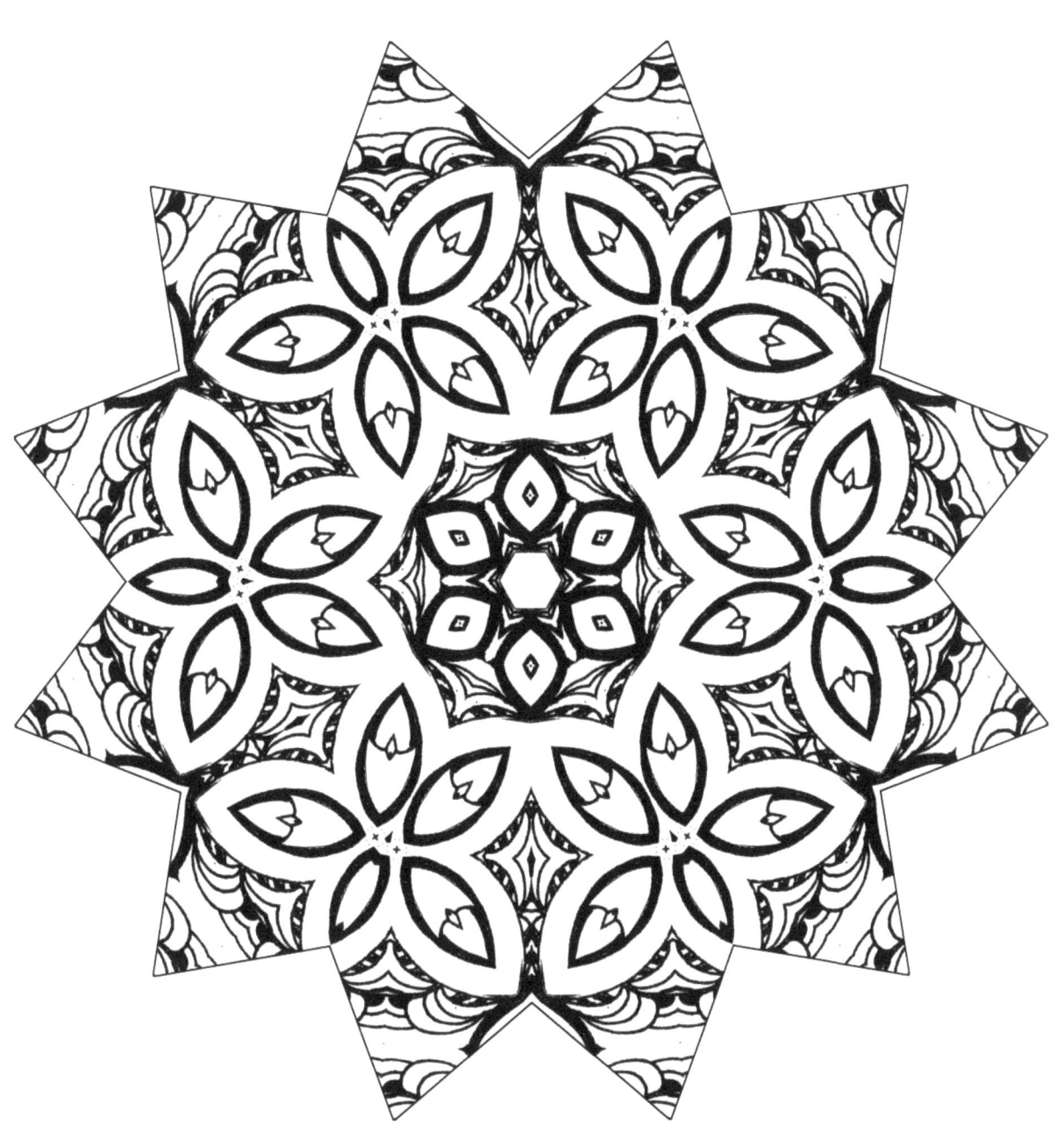

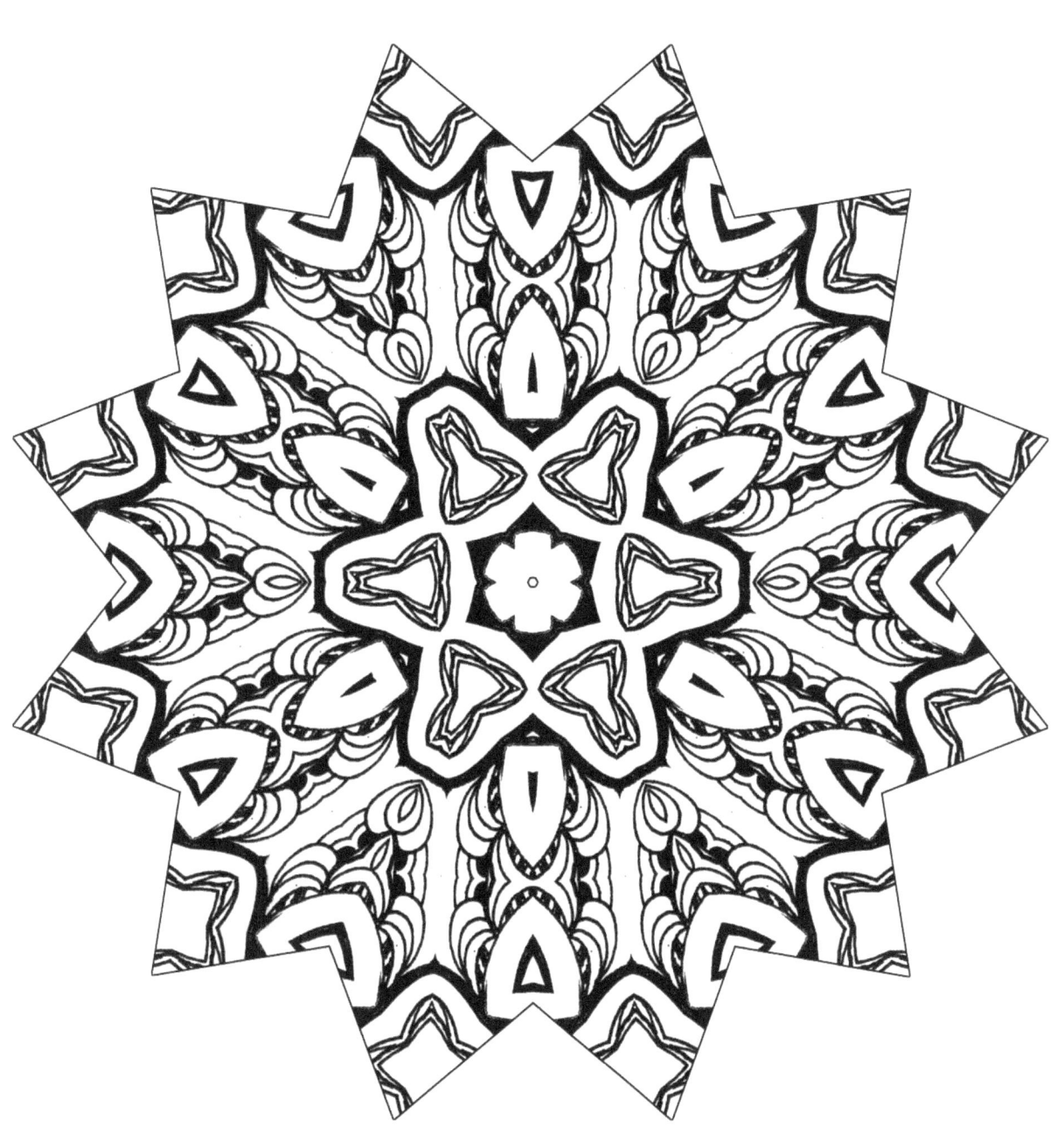

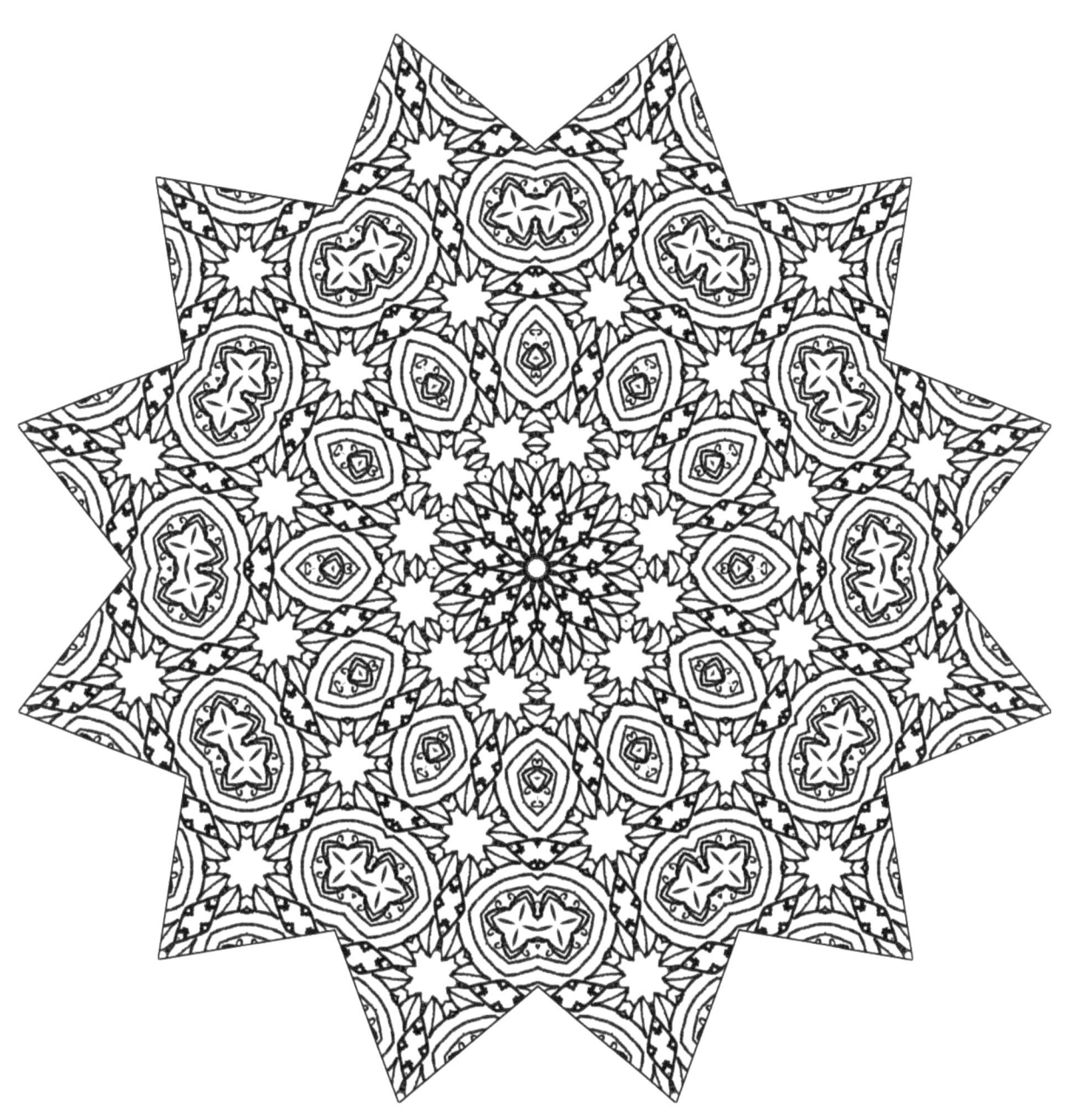

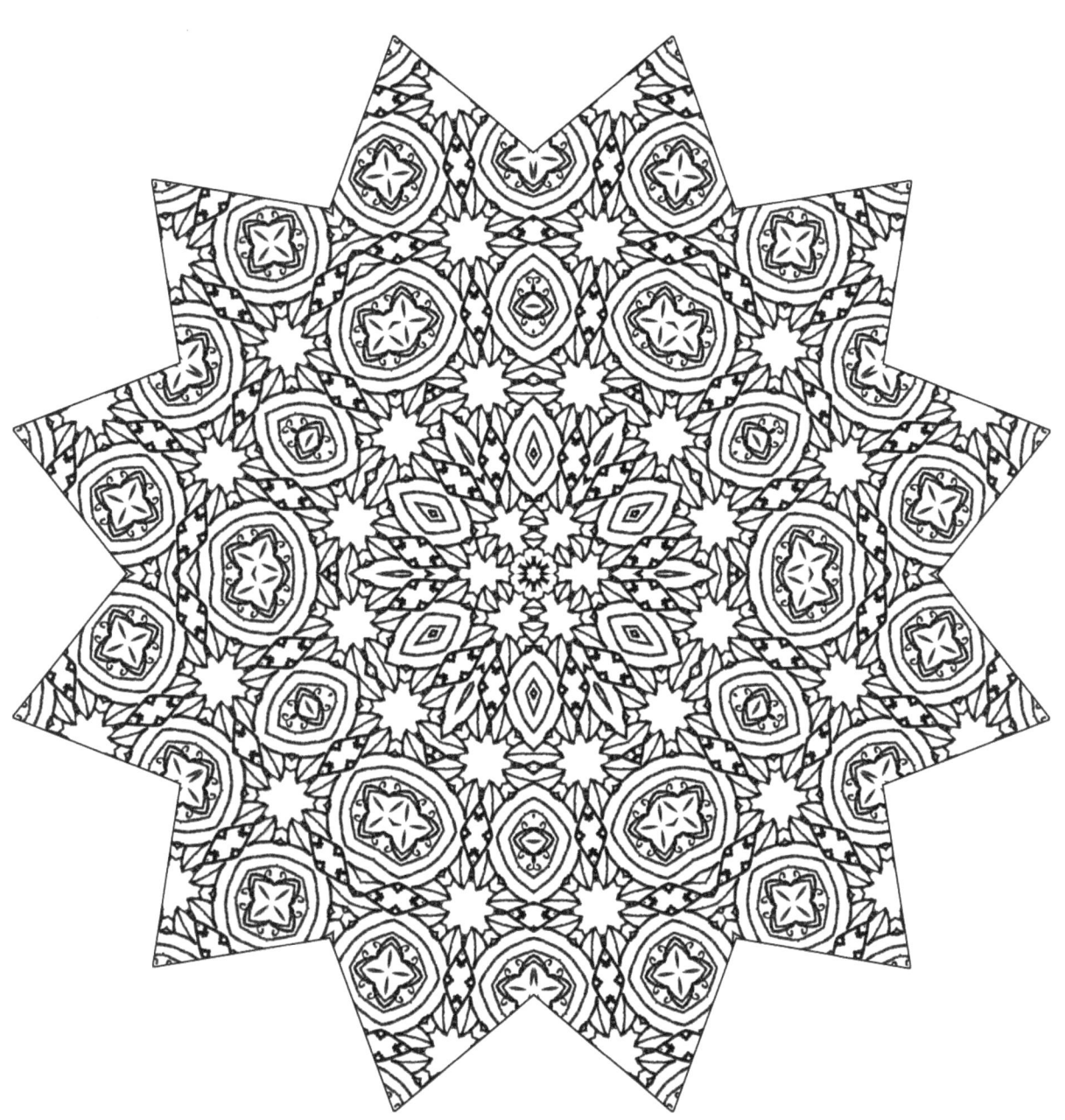

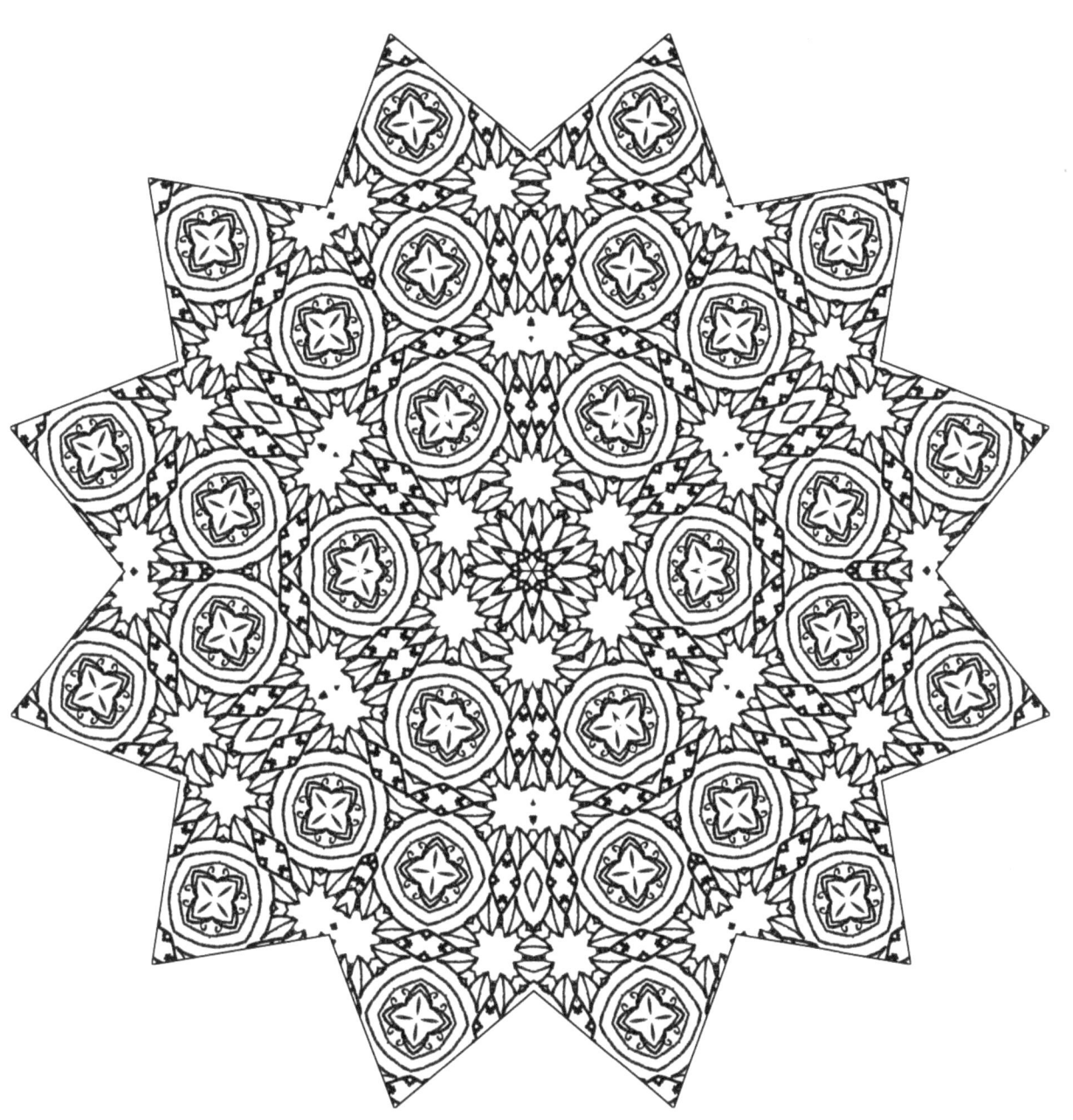

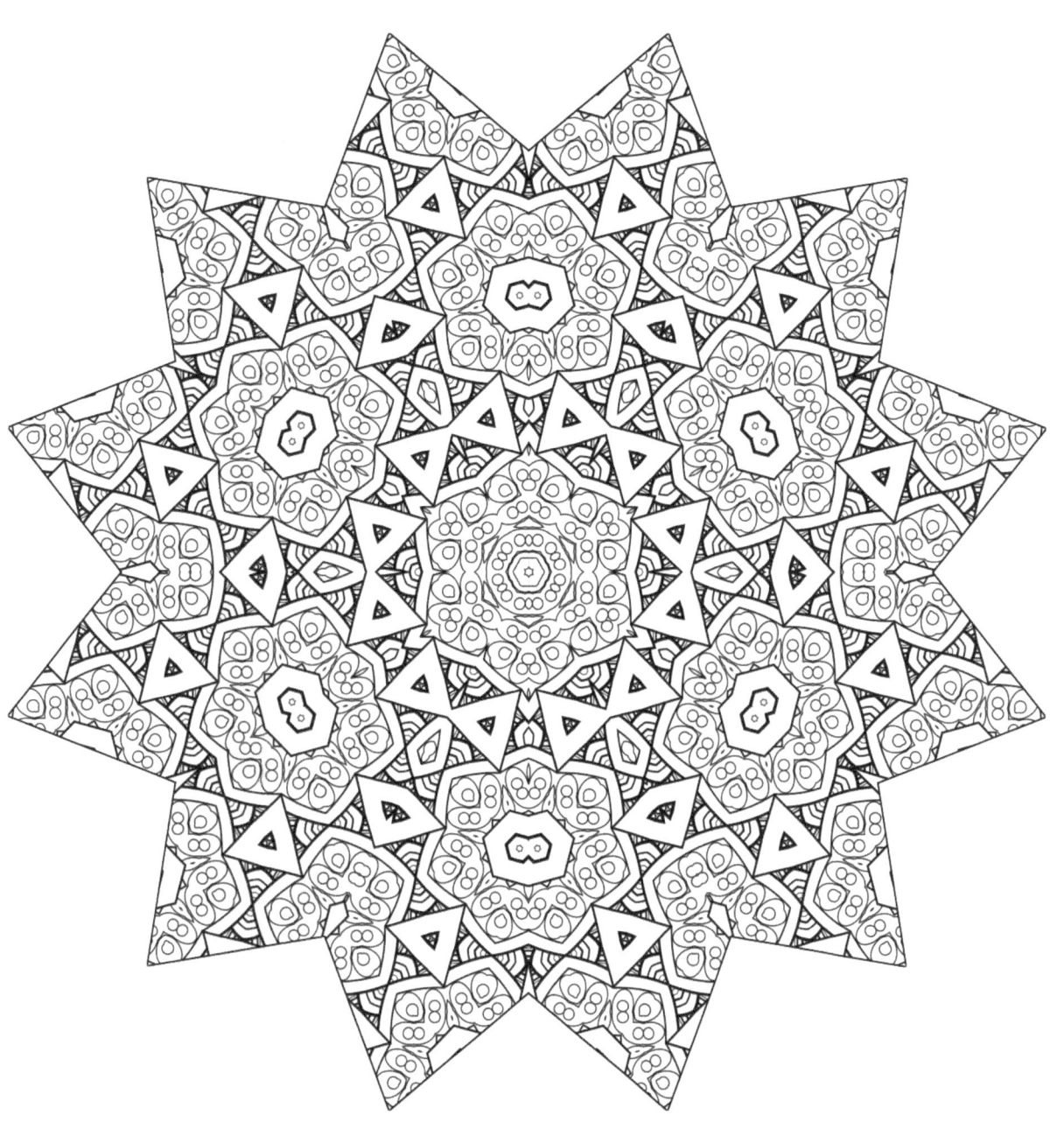

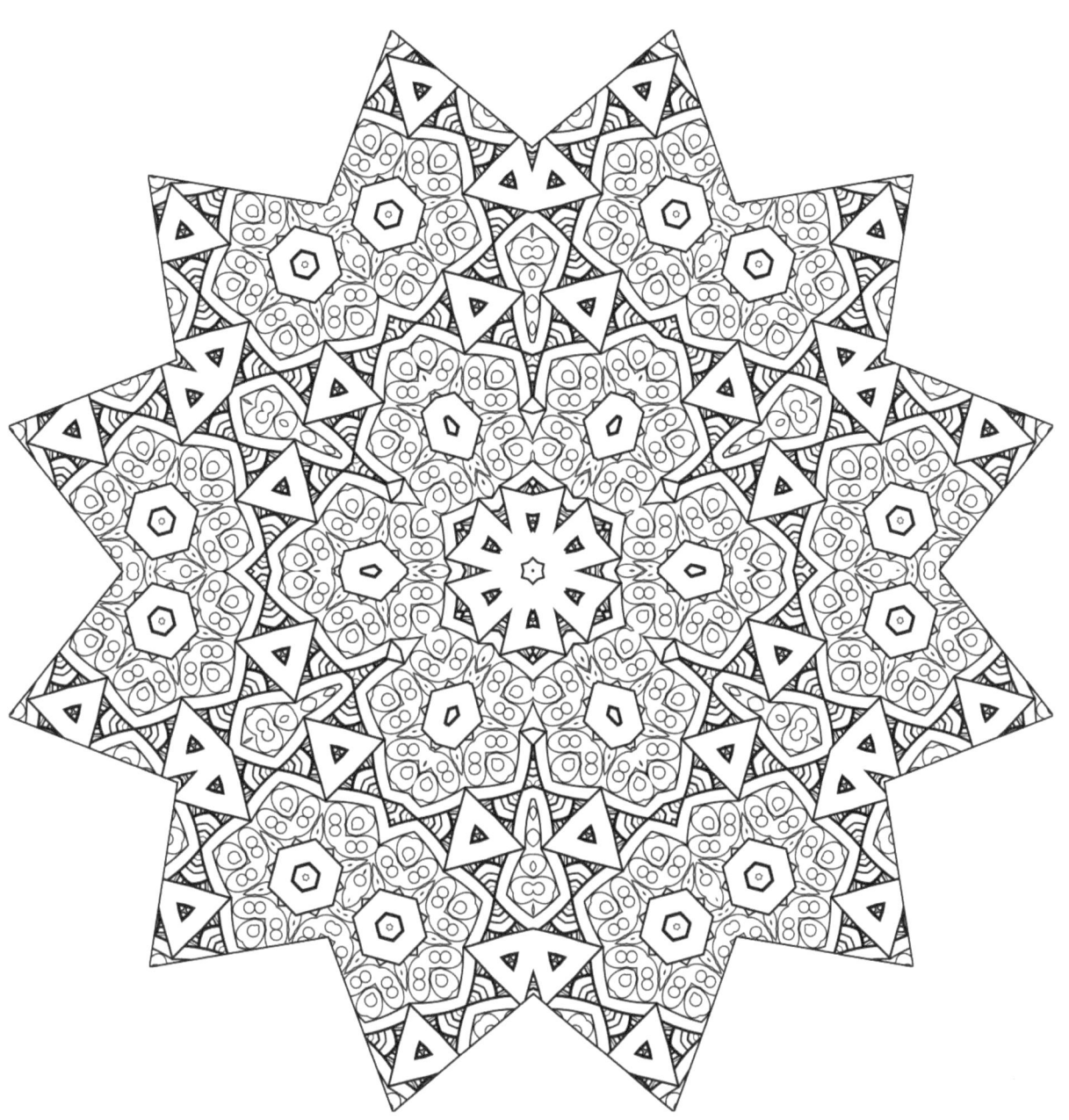

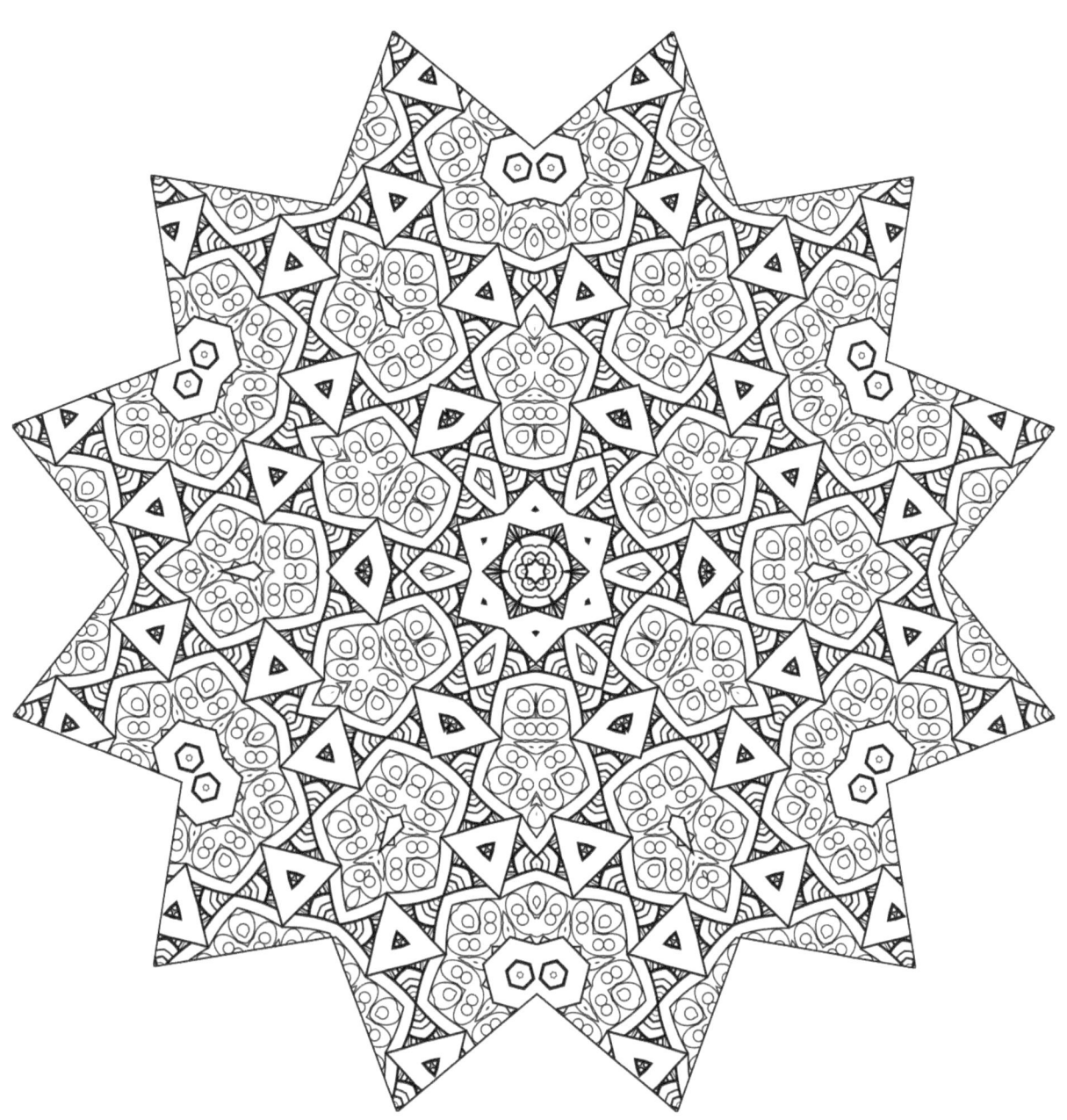

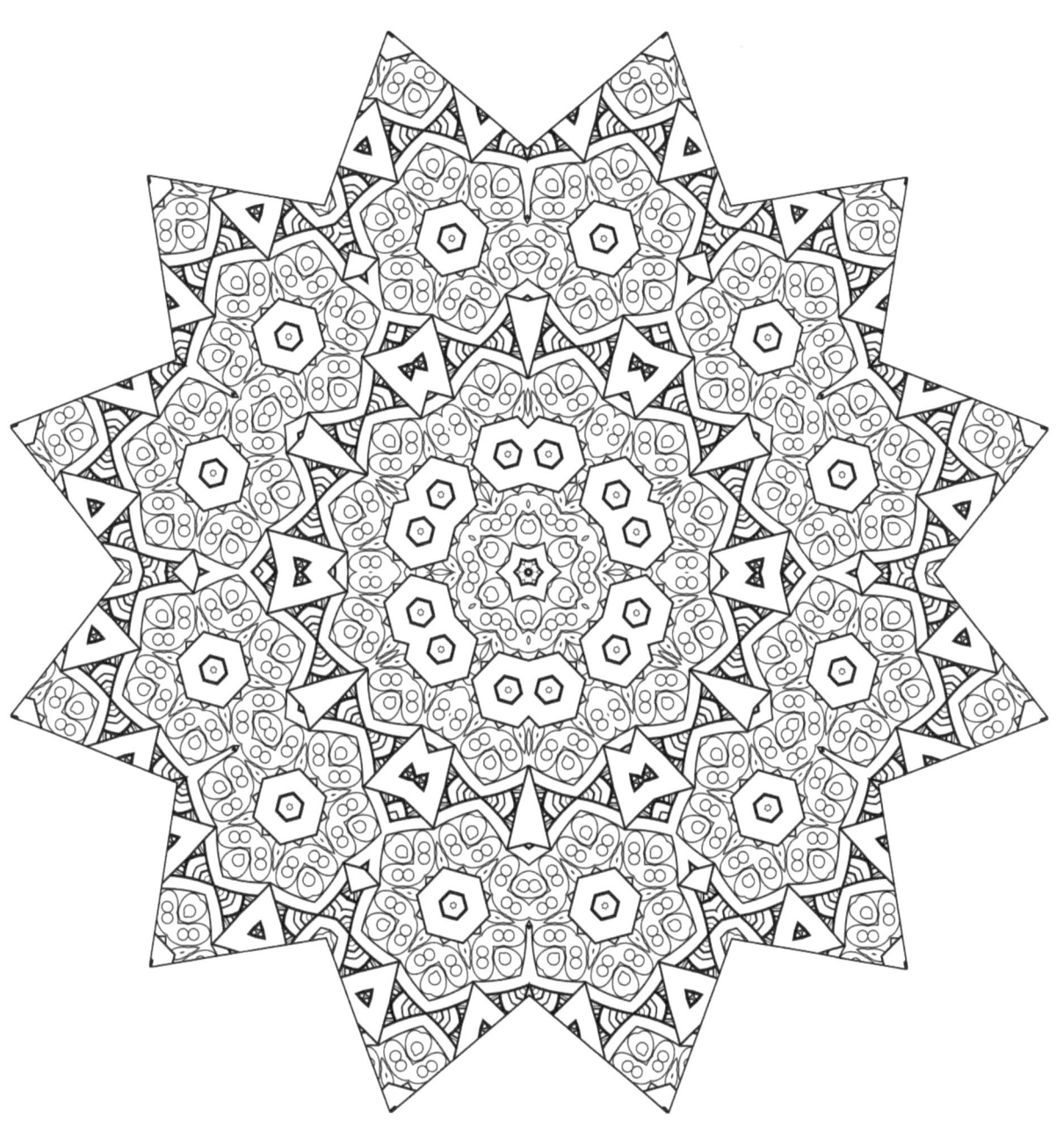

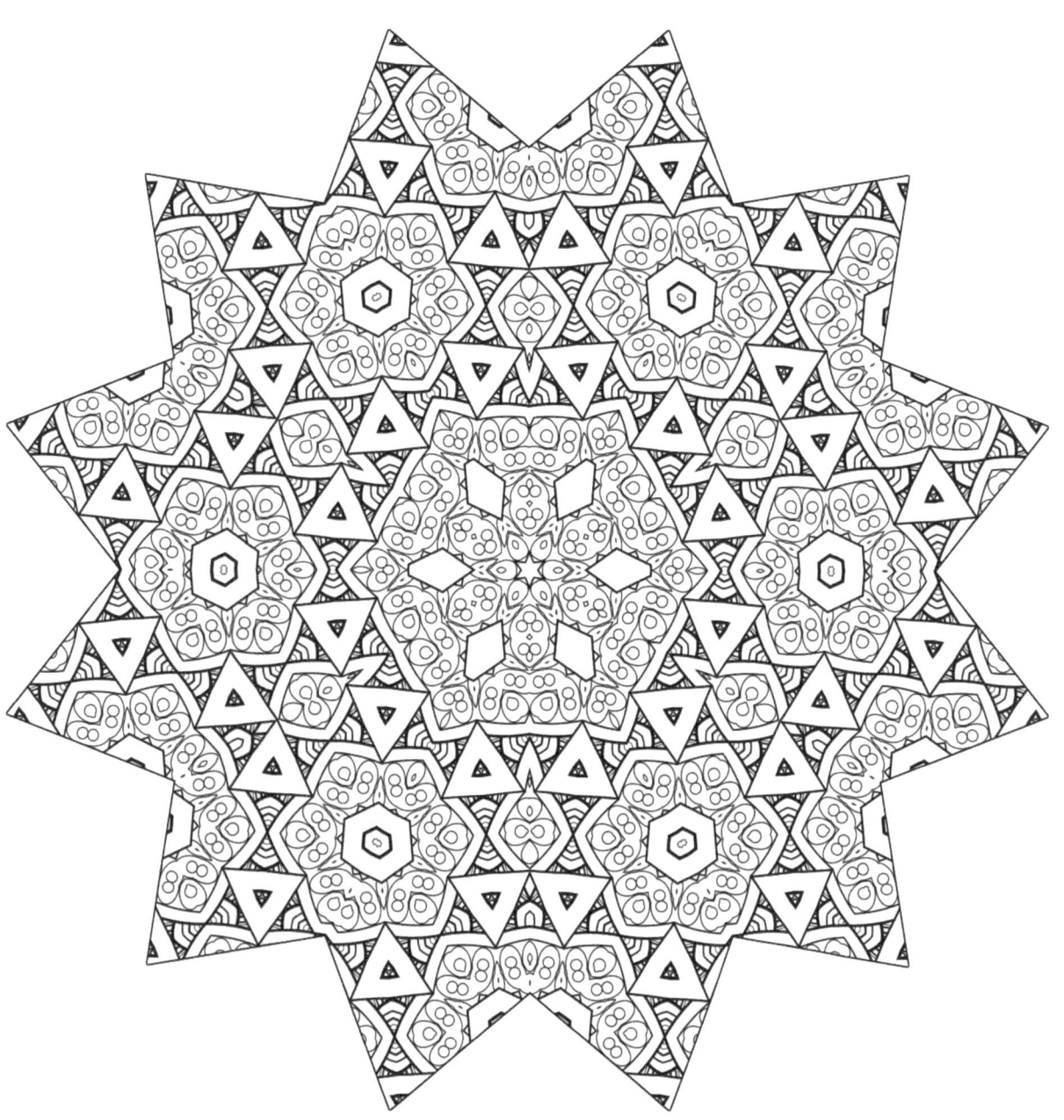

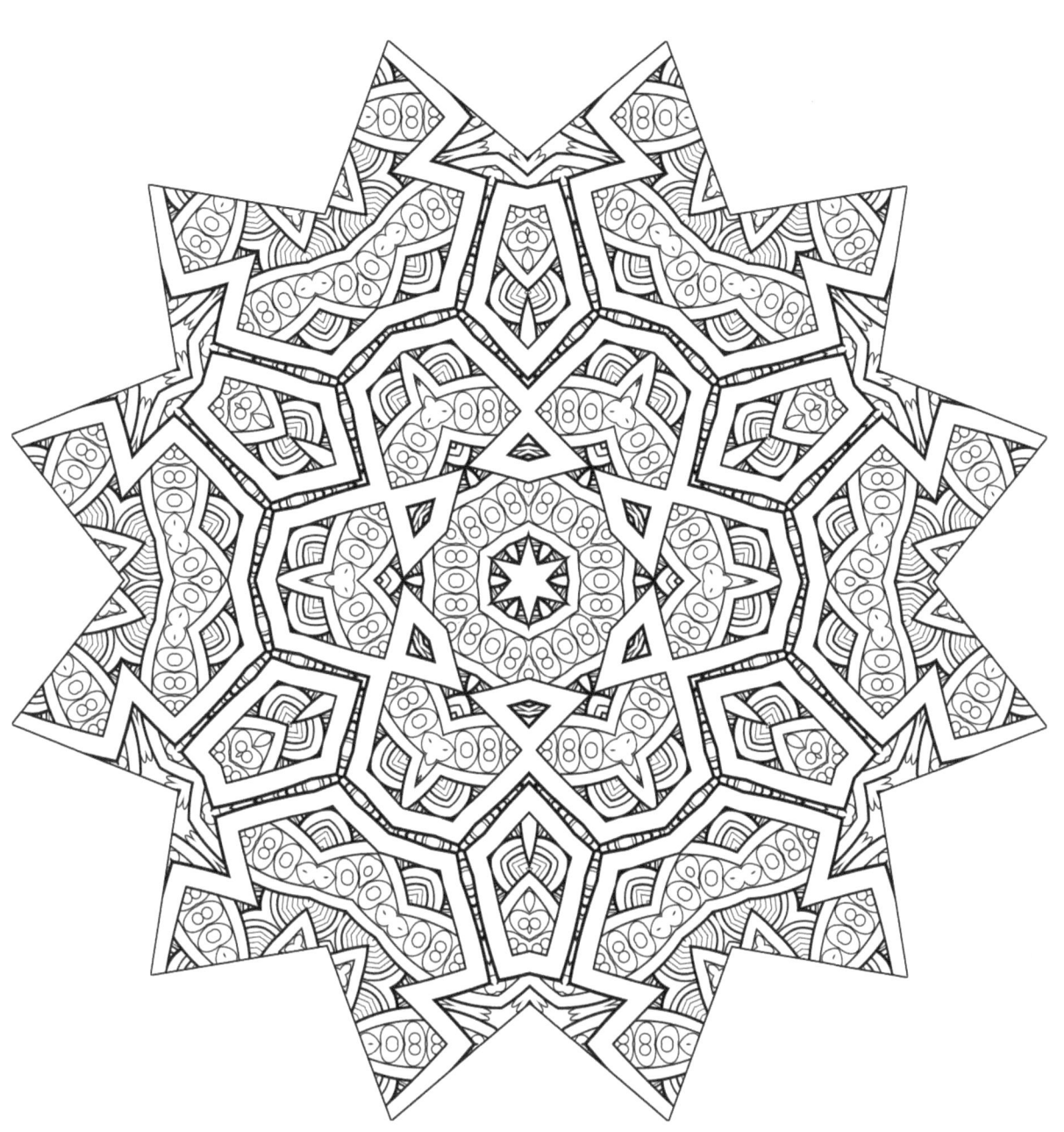

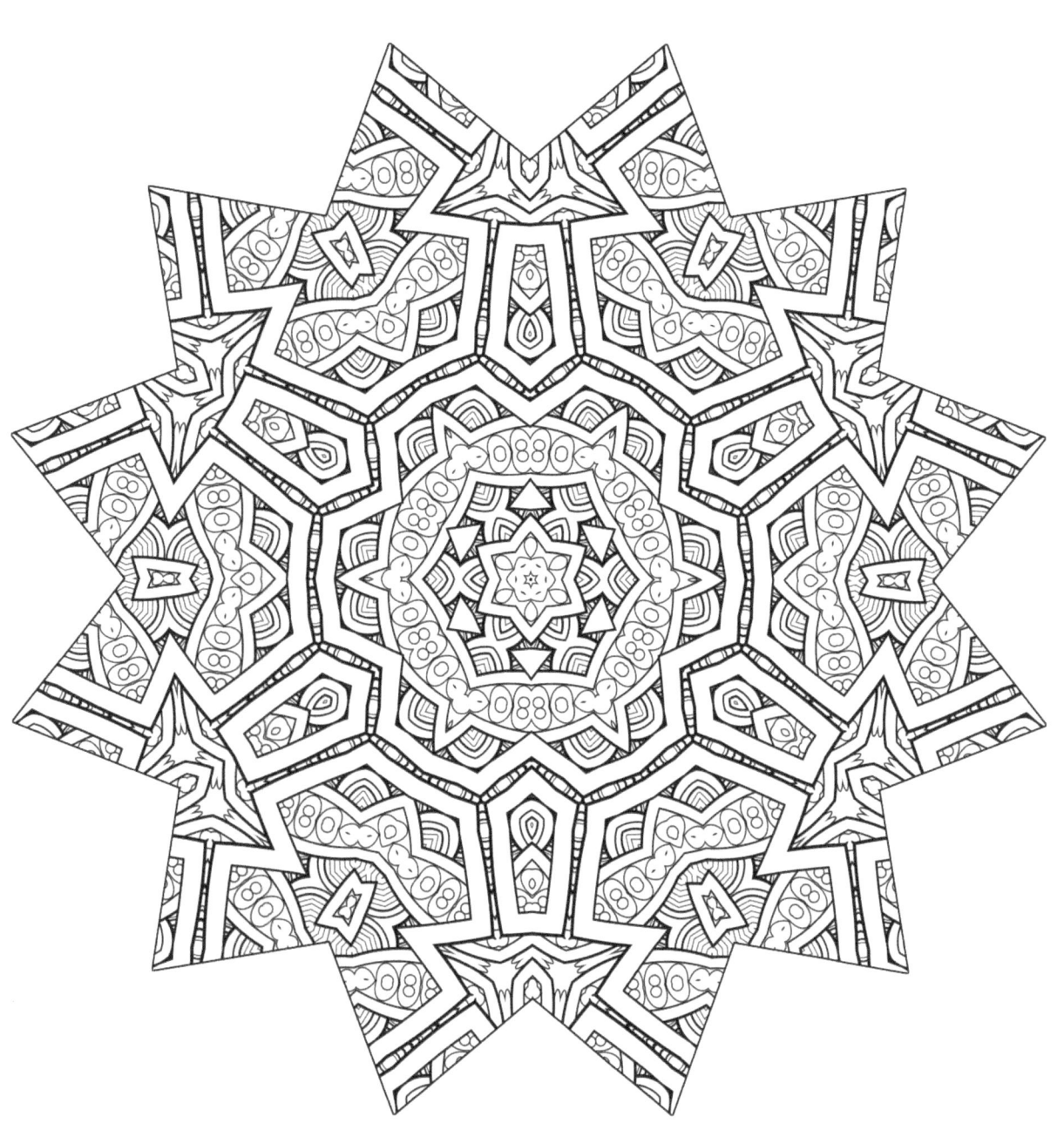

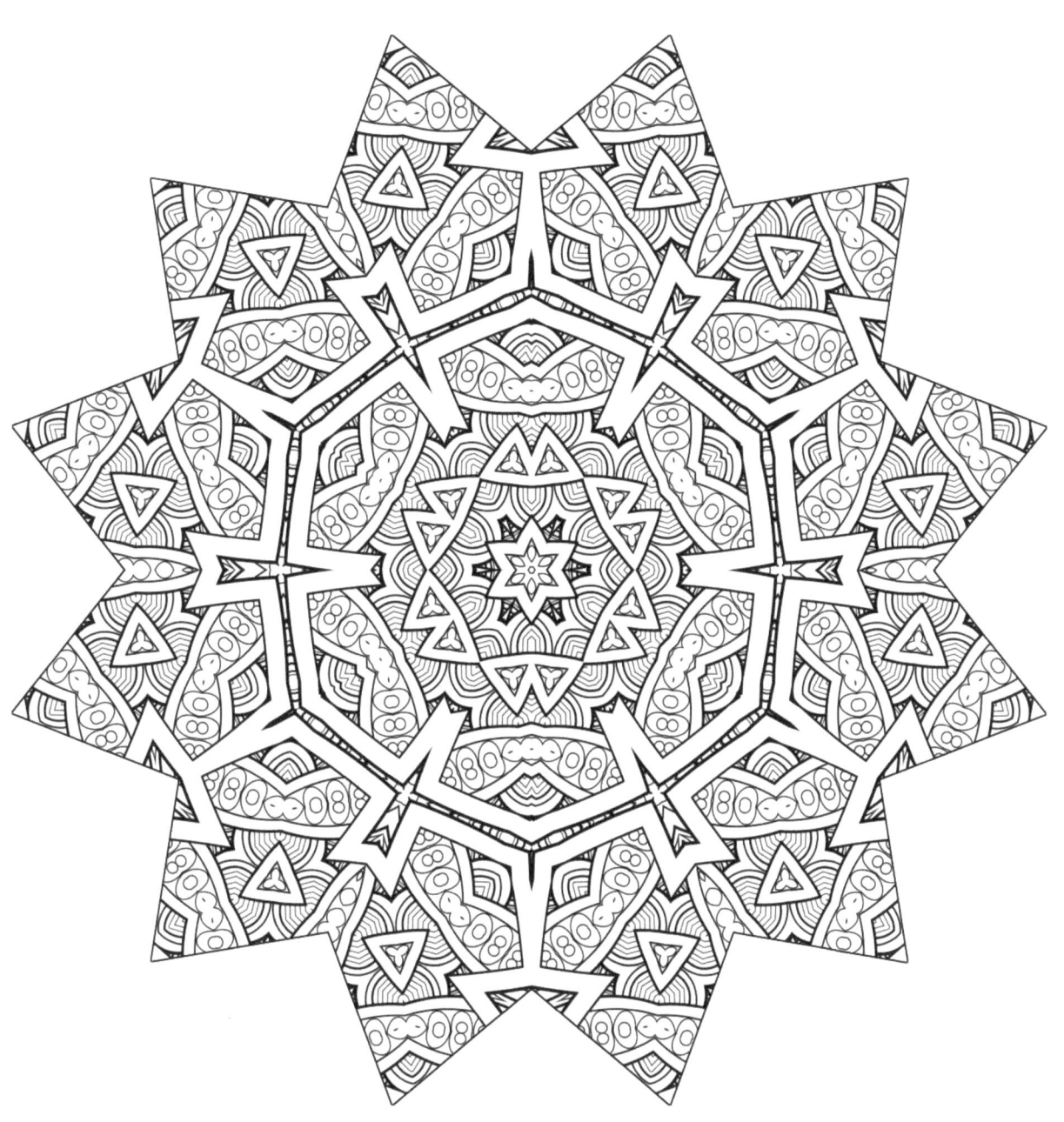

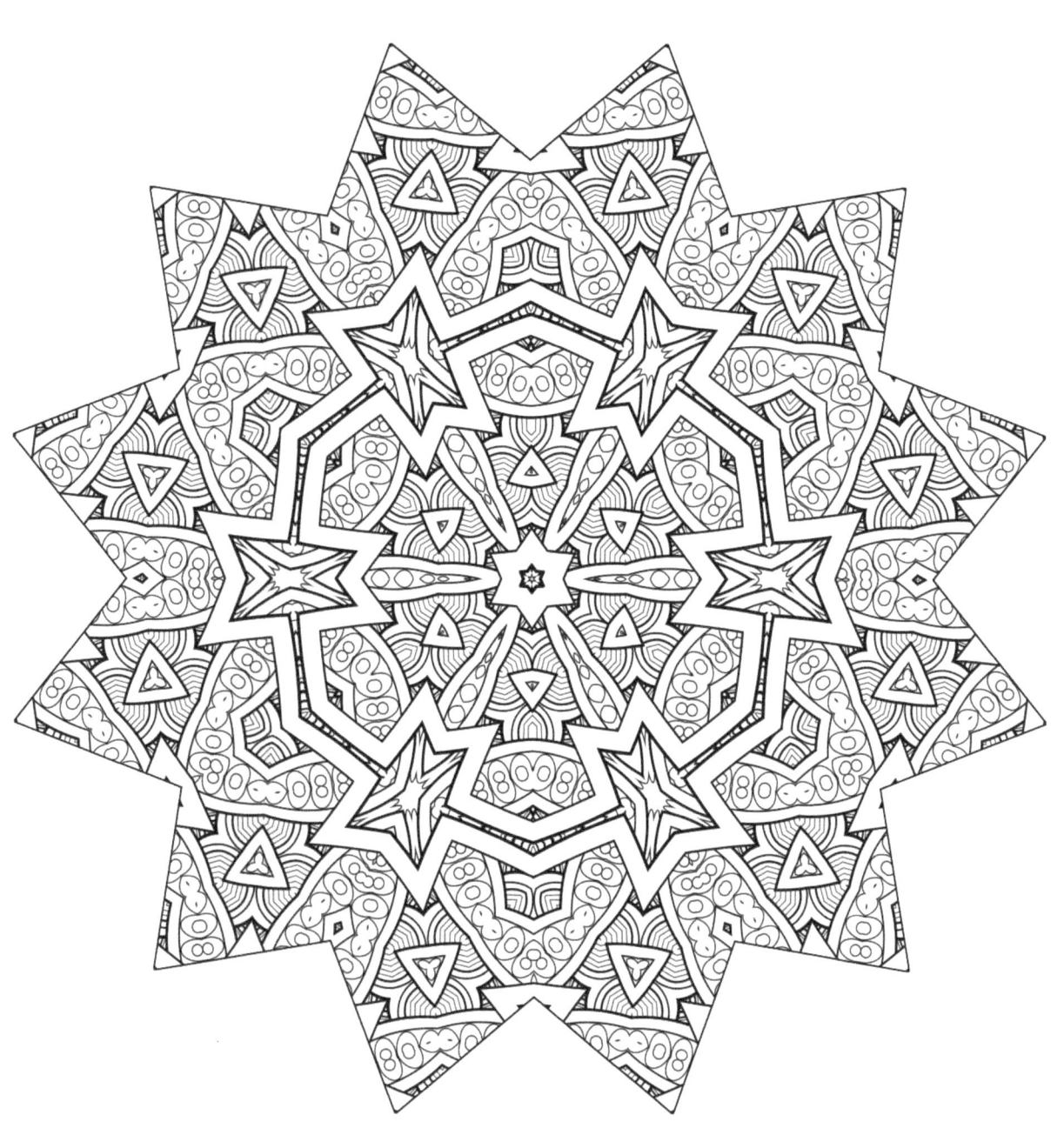

Health and Therapeutic Uses

Coloring books have seen wide application in the health professions as educational tools. One nurse, trying to limit the trauma of child surgery, described in an academic publication how the use of a coloring book "might help [the child] to understand what was going to happen to him." They are also used in rehabilitation of accident victims to aid recovery of hand-eye coordination, and they are used with autistic children both for entertainment and for their soothing effect. In some cases, coloring books were used to explain complicated medical conditions to children. One of the appeals of adult coloring books is that they help users relax and de-stress.

Coloring is a great way to explore your creativity — it's easy, inexpensive and you don't have to know how to draw. The 10 to 20 minutes you spend coloring — an image that gives you a sense of satisfaction can have a positive ripple effect throughout your day.

Coloring Books for Adults

Coloring is an activity that we tend to associate with children. As we grow older, we put aside our crayons and colored pencils in favor of more respectable writing utensils like pens and highlighters. However, it turns out coloring can be beneficial for adults — namely for its de-stressing power.

The practice generates wellness, quietness and also stimulates brain areas related to motor skills, the senses, and creativity. In fact, publishers have lately been launching coloring books specifically for adults. The trend is alive and well in countries in Europe and North America. Most recently, in Spain, the publication Espasa published Coloréitor, with illustrations by well-known cartoonist Forges.

(HuffPost Spain. Translation by Isaura Camós Gibert)

www.ingramcontent.com/pod-product-compliance
Lightning Source LLC
Chambersburg PA
CBHW051213220526
45473CB00003B/1019